CRAZY KNOCK-KNOCK JOKES
FOR KIDS WHO LOVE CATS

250+ SILLY AND SMART KNOCK-KNOCK JOKES FOR CLEVER KIDS
- A HILARIOUS GAME AND ACTIVITY BOOK FOR ALL THE FAMILY

FUNNY CRITTERS CAT BOOKS FOR KIDS

CRAZY CAT KNOCK-KNOCK JOKES FOR KIDS WHO LOVE CATS

250+ Silly and Smart Knock-Knock Jokes for Clever Kids– A Hilarious Game And Activity Book for All the Family, And a Funny Cat Book for Kids (8-12)

By Funny Critters Cat Books for Kids--

Copyright © 2022 -

All rights reserved. No part of this book may be reproduced in any form or by any means without permission in writing from the author. Please read the full disclaimer at the end of this book

I KNOW YOU LOVE CATS…

I KNOW YOU LOVE BOOKS

WOULDN'T YOU LIKE TO READ MORE FUN BOOKS ABOUT CATS?

FOR FREE…?

WHY NOT JOIN MY FAN CLUB?

SEE ALL THE DETAILS ON THE NEXT PAGE…

TABLE OF CONTENTS

Is That A Knock At The Door? -------------------7

Dear Parents, ---8

Hey, Kids! --- 10

Are You Ready?--------------------------------- 12

Here We Go….! ---------------------------------- 12

That's All "Fur" Now! ---------------------------145

Did You Like This Book? -----------------------147

Want To Read Other Funny Cat Books? ---148

Disclaimer ---151

Is That a Knock at the Door?

Better open up—it might be a cat waiting to tell you a funny knock-knock joke!

Kids and cat lovers of all ages can enjoy the 250 paw-some jokes in the pages of this book!

Spend time with your loved ones and make them laugh at the funny puns and cat antics that can be found in the knock-knock jokes collected here.

Enjoy twists on old classics and some totally new jokes that are sure to keep everyone entertained!

Dear Parents,

You can use this book to share the joy of knock-knock jokes and cats with your kids. Read these interactive question-and-answer jokes with them for some laugh-out-loud bonding time that can bring you all closer together.

Books like these can help bring families closer together, unlike sitting in front of the TV or spending time on the phone or tablet! Or, your kids can read this book by themselves, and it will keep them entertained for hours! They'll also get a kick out of sharing these jokes with their friends or siblings, which can brighten their day and banish boredom. What's more, the wordplay in knock-knock jokes can help stretch their brains and enhance their language skills.

This book is the purr-fect companion for long family road trips, school vacations, family get-togethers, rainy afternoons, snow days, or any time you find yourself wondering how to keep your kids occupied!

Happy Reading!!

--The Team at Funny Critters Cat Books for Kids

Hey, Kids!

Share these jokes with your friends, parents, or siblings! We guarantee you'll have hours of fun with these entertaining gags!

Every joke follows the same format, so it's easy to get into the rhythm. You say: "Knock-knock!" Your friend says: "Who's there?" And then the joke begins! Once you read the final line, your friends and family will be howling with laughter.

Or, you can take turns reading the jokes out loud and be surprised by the cat-tacular punch lines at the end. Telling these jokes or listening to these jokes—both are a blast!

No matter how you use this book, you'll be sure to have a fun time and laugh along with your friends and family! So, practice your funny cat voices - Meow!" "Hiss!" "Purr!" and get started. You and your friends might fall out of your chair laughing—so try to land on your feet! Unlike cats, you don't have nine lives…

ARE YOU READY? HERE WE GO….!

Knock-Knock!

Who's there?

Annie.

Annie who?

Annie body here who can lend a cat some money for cat food?

Knock-Knock!

Who's there?

Cat!

Cat who?

Just how many talking cats do you know?!

Knock-Knock!

Who's there?

Fred.

Fred who?

Fred I got the wrong house, pawfully sorry!

Knock-Knock!

Who's there?

Fur.

Fur who?

Fur Pete's sake, let me in!

Knock-Knock!

Who's there?

A cat whose paws can't reach the doorbell!

Knock-Knock!

Who's there?

Meow, meow.

Meow-meow, who?

Meow you doing?!

Knock-Knock!

Who's there?

Ida.

Ida who?

Ida-appreciate it if you'd let me nap on your couch!

Knock-Knock!

Who's there?

Me.

Me who?

Me-ow!

Knock-Knock!

Who's there?

Cats go.

Cats go who?

Of course not, cats go meow!

Knock-Knock!

Who's there?

Al.

Al who?

Al be back in a minute with some friends – can you keep the door open!

Knock-Knock!

Who's there?

Paw.

Paw who?

Paw-lease open the door!

Knock-Knock!

Who's there?

Cash.

Cash who?

I don't like cashews, but I'd love some salmon!

Knock-Knock!

Who's there?

Dozen.

Dozen who?

Dozen some human want to cuddle with this cute cat?!

Knock-Knock!

Who's there?

Paw.

Paw who?

Paw-some, you're home! Please let me in.

Knock-Knock!

Who's there?

Pet.

Pet who?

Pet-er open that door. I'm losing my paw-tience!

Knock-Knock!

Who's there?

Says.

Says who?

Says me-ow!

Knock-Knock!

Who's there?

Gino.

Gino who?

Gino that cats don't like to wait? Let me in!

Knock-Knock!

Who's there?

Herd.

Herd who?

Herd you wanted a cat so I came right over!

Knock-Knock!

Who's there?

Bean.

Bean who?

Bean out here for so long, please open the door meow!

Knock-Knock!

Who's there?

Dishes.

Dishes who?

Dishes your cat, open up!

Knock-Knock!

Who's there?

Snow.

Snow who?

Snow time for questions. It's cold outside, meow!

Knock-Knock!

Who's there?

Paw.

Paw who?

Paw-don me, I'd like to come in!

Knock-Knock!

Who's there?

Litter.

Litter who?

I've litter-aly been scratching for an hour, please let me in!

Knock-Knock!

Who's there?

Noah.

Noah who?

Noah-a place where I can get some cat treats?

Knock-Knock!

Who's there?

Tail.

Tail who?

Tail me you have some cat treats. I'm hungry!

Knock-Knock!

Who's there?

Woo.

Woo who?

I'm feeling happy to see you too!

Knock-Knock!

Who's there?

Witches.

Witches who?

Witches the way to the cat food?!

Knock-Knock!

Who's there?

Water.

Water who?

Water you are waiting for, please open up meow!

Knock-Knock!

Who's there?

Donut.

Donut who?

Donut stand in my way! Just let me in!

Knock-Knock!

Who's there?

Avery.

Avery who?

Avery adorable kitten who wants to come inside!

Knock-Knock!

Who's there?

Whisker.

Whisker who?

Whisker me into your house, meow!

Knock-Knock!

Who's there?

Mouse.

Mouse who?

Mouse, you be so nosy? Just let me in!

Knock-Knock!

Who's there?

Thumping.

Thumping who?

Thumping thmall, furry, and cute ith on your porch!

Knock-Knock!

Who's there?

Some bunny.

Some bunny who?

Some bunny has eaten all my cat treats!

Knock-Knock!

Who's there?

Gorilla.

Gorilla who?

Gorilla nice fish for me to eat--salmon, if you have it!

Knock-Knock!

Who's there?

Hen.

Hen who?

Hen will you let me in, meow?! My paws are tired from knocking!

Knock-Knock!

Who's there?

Ivan.

Ivan who?

Ivan-a nice home, please bring me inside! Me-ow...

Knock-Knock!

Who's there?

Hiss.

Hiss who?

Hiss too hot out, let me rest my paws inside!

Knock-Knock!

Who's there?

Anita.

Anita who?

Anita more cat food, please let me in!

Knock-Knock!

Who's there?

Our fur.

Our fur who?

Oh no, our fur-got!

Knock-Knock!

Who's there?

Boo.

Boo who?

Don't cry, I'm just a little cat! I won't hurt you!

Knock-Knock!

Who's there?

My fur.

My fur who?

My fur-end told me you've got some cool cat toys. Let me in so I can play with them!

Knock-Knock!

Who's there?

Aida.

Aida who?

Aida too much fish for lunch and my tummy hurts!

Knock-Knock!

Who's there?

4 + 4.

4 +4 who?

Oh, is it time to 8, meow?!

Knock-Knock!

Who's there?

Leash.

Leash who?

Leash me explain – I knock, you open the door. Got it?

Knock-Knock!

Who's there?

Yowl.

Yowl who?

Yowl be sorry if you don't let me in! I'll dig up all the flowers in your garden!

Knock-Knock!

Who's there?

Tail.

Tail who?

Tail you later…

Knock-Knock!

Who's there?

Hugo.

Hugo who?

Hugo to the store and get me some treats, and I'll go inside and sleep!

Knock-Knock!

Who's there?

Broken claw!

Broken claw who?

Oh, never mind---it's pointless!

Knock-Knock!

Who's there?

Mew.

Mew who?

Mew-sic is my life, I listen to it all the time!

Knock-Knock!

Who's there?

Tabby.

Tabby who?

Tabby birthday! Here's a bird I found outside for you, meow!

Knock-Knock!

Who's there?

Calico.

Calico who?

Calico to the store for some cat treats?!

Knock-Knock!

Who's there?

Hair.

Hair who?

Hair I am, please let me in, meow!

Knock-Knock!

Who's there?

Fur.

Fur who?

Fur-get it, I'll go somewhere else!

Knock-Knock!

Who's there?

Tooth.

Tooth who?

It's tooth hurty, time to go to the vet!

Knock-Knock!

Who's there?

Carrie.

Carrie who?

Carrie me to my cat bed, please!

Knock-Knock!

Who's there?

Tuna.

Tuna who?

Tuna the handle and let me in, meow!

Knock-Knock!

Who's there?

Butter.

Butter who?

Butter let me in before my paws freeze off!

Knock-Knock!

Who's there?

Poodle.

Poodle who?

Poodle little fish in my cat food, please!

Knock-Knock!

Who's there?

Soup.

Soup who?

Soupercat, here to save the day!

Knock-Knock!

Who's there?

Little old kitty!

Little old kitty who?

I didn't know you could yodel!

Knock-Knock!

Who's there?

Fur.

Fur who?

Fur-tunately you're here. Let me in!

Knock-Knock!

Who's there?

Watch.

Watch who?

Bless you, meow!

Knock-Knock!

Who's there?

Hiss.

Hiss who?

Here's a hiss-ue, so blow your nose!

Knock-Knock!

Who's there?

Gus.

Gus who?

Gus where I left my hairball? Right on your pillow!

Knock-Knock!

Who's there?

Olive.

Olive who?

Olive kibble. You got any?

Knock-Knock!

Who's there?

Dwayne.

Dwayne who?

Dwayne the bath, I hate water!

Knock-Knock!

Who's there?

Ben.

Ben who?

Ben knocking all day, now my paw hurts!

Knock-Knock!

Who's there?

Howl.

Howl who?

Howl I know your food is any good if you don't let me taste some?

Knock-Knock!

Who's there?

Alpine.

Alpine who?

Alpine away if you don't let me in! Meeooowww!

Knock-Knock!

Who's there?

Lion.

Lion who?

Lion is wrong! You should always tell the truth!

Knock-Knock!

Who's there?

Ivanna.

Ivanna who?

Ivanna step on your keyboard! Xxxxxxxxxxjksafkkkkkkk

Knock-Knock!

Who's there?

Igor.

Igor who?

Igor you?! Never! I just didn't see you…

Knock-Knock!

Who's there?

Luke.

Luke who?

Luke out the window, it's so sunny! Come out and play!

Knock-Knock!

Who's there?

Ice cream.

Ice cream who?

I scream when humans ask me dumb questions!

Knock-Knock!

Who's there?

Theodore.

Theodore who?

Theodore wasn't open which is why I'm knocking!

Knock-Knock!

Who's there?

Scott.

Scott who?

The door Scott on something. Can you help me get it open?

Knock-Knock!

Who's there?

Ears.

Ears who?

Ears a hairball just for you! I hope you like it!

Knock-Knock!

Who's there?

Alex.

Alex who?

Alex you again… Please, can you let me in?

Knock-Knock!

Who's there?

Turnip.

Turnip who?

Turnip the volume on the music, I can't hear it out here, meow!

Knock-Knock!

Who's there?

Juno.

Juno who?

Juno you have a lovely house... Can I come inside?

Knock-Knock!

Who's there?

Accord.

Accord who?

Accord is what you use to charge your phone… I thought you'd know that!

Knock-Knock!

Who's there?

Amish.

Amish who?

Well, I guess amish you too, meow!

Knock-Knock.

Who's there?

Les.

Les who?

Les get to the point--just open up and let me in!

Knock-Knock!

Who's there?

Wooden shoe.

Wooden shoe who?

Wooden shoe like to know, meow!

Knock-Knock!

Who's there?

Cock-a-doodle.

Cock-a-doodle who?

It's morning! Wake up and feed me, please!

Knock-Knock!

Who's there?

Olive.

Olive who?

Olive next door, but I heard you have a good scratching post over here!

Knock-Knock!

Who's there?

Amy.

Amy who?

Amy-fraid a scary dog is following me. Can I come inside?

Knock-Knock.

Who's there?

Surrey.

Surrey who?

Surrey I ran out, but the door was open! Now let me back in!

Knock-Knock!

Who's there?

A cat burglar!

A cat burglar who?

Oh, whoops. Cat burglars shouldn't knock – I should have just broken in!

Knock-Knock!

Who's there?

Hurricane!

Hurricane who?

Hurricane you open the door? It's so windy out here!

Knock-Knock!

Who's there?

Purr.

Purr who?

Purr-sonally, I think you should invite me in for dinner!

Knock-Knock!

Who's there?

Otto.

Otto who?

Otto let me in and stop wasting my time!

Knock-Knock!

Who's there?

Abed.

Abed who?

Abed you can't run as fast I can!

Knock-Knock!

Who's there?

Figs.

Figs who?

Figs this cat door, it's stuck!

Knock-Knock!

Who's there?

Ketchup.

Ketchup who?

Ketchup with me and I'll let you pet me!

Knock-Knock!

Who's there?

Lessee.

Lessee who?

Lessee if you've got a nice sofa inside I can sit on!

Knock-Knock!

Who's there?

Salmon.

Salmon who?

Salmon doesn't have a last name--but it does sound delicious!

Knock-Knock!

Who's there?

Comb.

Comb who?

Comb here and play with me, meow!

Knock-Knock!

Who's there?

Fangs.

Fangs who?

Fangs for scratching behind my ears!

Knock-Knock!

Who's there?

Glib.

Glib who?

Glib me some attention now, or I'll knock this flowerpot over!

Knock-Knock!

Who's there?

Sigh.

Sigh who?

Sigh-n for this package, please!

Knock-Knock!

Who's there?

Bacon.

Bacon who?

Bacon-siderate and invite me inside!

Knock-Knock!

Who's there?

Doris.

Doris who?

Doris locked, and I forgot my key!

Knock-Knock!

Who's there?

Luck.

Luck who?

Luck out here, I'm waiting for you to let me in!

Knock-Knock!

Who's there?

Gladys.

Gladys who?

Gladys is nearly time for dinner. What are we having?

Knock-Knock!

Who's there?

Hiss.

Hiss who?

Hiss-torically cats were treated like royalty. I should be, too! Lead me to my throne...

Knock-Knock!

Who's there?

Gif.

Gif who?

Gif me a break, and just let me in!

Knock-Knock!

Who's there?

Mike.

Mike who?

My collar fell off! Have you seen it?

Knock-Knock!

Who's there?

Um.

Um who?

Um sleepy, let me in so I can take a nap in your bed!

Knock-Knock!

Who's there?

Aisle.

Aisle who?

Aisle be moving in later today. Just thought you'd like to know…

Knock-Knock!

Who's there?

Wire.

Wire who?

Wire you asking me, I'm just a cat!

Knock-Knock!

Who's there?

Radio.

Radio who?

Radio not it's time for me to come in!

Knock-Knock!

Who's there?

Alms.

Alms who?

Alm scared of dogs, so let me inside where I'll be safe!

Knock-Knock!

Who's there?

Fiddle.

Fiddle who?

Fiddle make you smile, I guess you can pet me!

Knock-Knock!

Who's there?

Harry.

Harry who?

Harry up and clean the litter box so I can come in and use it!

Knock-Knock!

Who's there?

Paws in.

Paws in who?

Paws in before you open the door is just wastin' my time!

Knock-Knock!

Who's there?

My tea.

My tea who?

My tea-ail is at the end of me!

Knock-Knock!

Who's there?

Masking.

Masking who?

Masking you to donate money to the Cat Charity! It's for a good claws…

Knock-Knock!

Who's there?

Gato.

Gato who?

Gato say, you took long enough coming to the door!

Knock-Knock.

Who's there?

Abby.

Abby who?

Abby stung my nose, it hurts! Won't you take me to the vet?

Knock-Knock.

Who's there?

Cain.

Cain who?

Cain you tell me why this door still isn't open!?

Knock-Knock.

Who's there?

Watts.

Watts who?

Watts taking so long? Open up, meow!

Knock-Knock.

Who's there?

Hour.

Hour who?

Hour paws are tired, so let us all rest inside!

Knock-Knock.

Who's there?

Mascara.

Mascara who?

Mascara-dy cat! Let me in where there are no dogs!

Knock-Knock!

Who's there?

Ken.

Ken who?

Ken we watch some funny cat videos together?

Knock-Knock.

Who's there?

Chat.

Chat who?

Chat, chat, chat, that's all you do! Just let me inside!

Knock-Knock.

Who's there?

Juicy.

Juicy who?

Juicy a mouse run by here? Better let me check inside!

Knock-Knock.

Who's there?

Aaron.

Aaron who?

Aaron you the one who lives here? Open the door!

Knock-Knock.

Who's there?

Puma.

Puma who?

Puma food bowl out here so I don't have to come inside!

Knock-Knock.

Who's there?

Flew.

Flew who?

Flew-fy cats with lots of fur get too hot in the sun. Bring me some cold water!

Knock-Knock.

Who's there?

Leo.

Leo who?

Leo-nly thing I want is for you to open the door—and gimme a scratch behind the ears.

Knock-Knock.

Who's there?

Moustache.

Moustache who?

Moustache you a question... Do you have a nice cat bed inside?

Knock-Knock.

Who's there?

Lemming.

Lemming who?

Lemming come inside, I've been out here hunting all day!

Knock-Knock!

Who's there?

Distress.

Distress who?

Distress is cute, but do you have a hat to match?

84

Knock-Knock.

Who's there?

Island.

Island who?

Island on my feet whenever I fall!

Knock-Knock.

Who's there?

Ken.

Ken who?

Ken you let me in and lend me a warm blanket?

Knock-Knock.

Who's there?

Dough.

Dough who?

Dough not forget to let me in, meow!

Knock-Knock.

Who's there?

Mikey.

Mikey who?

Mikey got lost. Let me in!

Knock-Knock.

Who's there?

Isaac.

Isaac who?

Isaac and tired waiting for you to let me inside!

Knock-Knock.

Who's there?

Idaho.

Idaho who?

Idaho-pe you'd open the door for a sweet little cat!

Knock-Knock.

Who's there?

Bali.

Bali who?

Bali-ve it or not, cats don't like to wait all day to be let in!

Knock-Knock.

Who's there?

Hairy.

Hairy who?

Hairy up, let me in before all my nine lives are up!

Knock-Knock.

Who's there?

Claw.

Claw who?

Clawfully rude of you to keep a cat waiting on the porch all day!

Knock-Knock.

Who's there?

Dew.

Dew who?

Dew you have any time to come out and play catch?

Knock-Knock.

Who's there?

Ant.

Ant who?

An-two seconds I'm going to start scratching at the door!

Knock-Knock.

Who's there?

Ion.

Ion who?

Ion a cool sports car. Wanna come for a drive?

Knock-Knock.

Who's there?

Eggs.

Eggs who?

Eggs-cuse me, could you fill out this survey about your cat's favorite food?

Knock-Knock.

Who's there?

Emma.

Emma who?

Emma tired cat, can I come in for a nap?

Knock-Knock.

Who's there?

Theo.

Theo who?

Theo-nly thing I want is a snack. Do you have one?

Knock-Knock.

Who's there?

Half.

Half who?

Half you heard about doors that open themselves – maybe you should get one?

Knock-Knock.

Who's there?

Alex.

Alex who?

Alex you nicely one more time--will you let me in to charge my cat phone?

Knock-Knock.

Who's there?

Dragon.

Dragon who?

Stop dragon your feet and open this door, meow!

Knock-Knock.

Who's there?

Star.

Star who?

I'm star-ving and I'd like some dinner!

Knock-Knock.

Who's there?

Bed.

Bed who?

Bed-er let me in or I'll meow here all day!

Knock-Knock.

Who's there?

Juan.

Juan who?

Juan can I come in? It's getting late, and we cats need our rest!

Knock-Knock.

Who's there?

Bottle.

Bottle who?

Bottle little yummy tuna, would you like some too?

Knock-Knock.

Who's there?

Wire.

Wire who?

Wire you telling jokes when you should just let me in!

Knock-Knock.

Who's there?

Cup.

Cup who?

Cup-ple of cute cats, waiting to come in!

Knock-Knock.

Who's there?

Purr.

Purr who?

Purr-haps you have some time to play? I brought my squeaky mouse toy!

Knock-Knock.

Who's there?

Candies.

Candies who?

Candies cats come in? We're hungry and cold!

Knock-Knock.

Who's there?

June.

June who?

June know how much cats hate to wait? Mee-oow!

Knock-Knock.

Who's there?

A knee.

A knee who?

A knee cups I can knock over in there? It's so much fun!

Knock-Knock.

Who's there?

Venice.

Venice who?

Venice is dinner ready? I'll come back then…

Knock-Knock!

Who's there?

Phillip.

Phillip who?

Phillip my bowl with food!

Knock-Knock.

Who's there?

Falafel.

Falafel who?

Falafel a branch and hurt my paw! Have a bandage?

Knock-Knock.

Who's there?

Utah.

Utah who?

Utah-lk too much, human! Stop yapping and open the door, meow!

Knock-Knock.

Who's there?

Sarah.

Sarah who?

Sarah a cat toy in your house that I can play with?

Knock-Knock.

Who's there?

Dakota.

Dakota who?

Dakota fur I have isn't enough to keep me warm! Let me lay by your fire!

Knock-Knock.

Who's there?

Canada.

Canada who?

Canada-g purr? No! That's why cats are better by fur!

Knock-Knock.

Who's there?

Missouri.

Missouri who?

Missouri to bother you, but can I come inside?

Knock-Knock.

Who's there?

Greece.

Greece who?

Greece the door, it's so squeaky it makes my ears hurt!

Knock-Knock.

Who's there?

Haiti.

Haiti who?

Haiti see your mail get chewed up.... Unless you let me in!

Knock-Knock.

Who's there?

Jamaica.

Jamaica who?

Jamaica me some tasty treats, please?

Knock-Knock.

Who's there?

Kenya.

Kenya who?

Kenya hurry up and get the jingle ball so we can play?

Knock-Knock.

Who's there?

Mali.

Mali who?

Mali-st favorite holiday is Halloween, it's too spooky!

Knock-Knock.

Who's there?

Norway.

Norway who?

Norway can I open this door! My paws can't grab the handle!

Knock-Knock.

Who's there?

Sweden.

Sweden who?

I'll Sweden the deal! I'll bring you a dead mouse if you let me in!

Knock-Knock.

Who's there?

Turkey.

Turkey who?

Turkey you gave me got lost! Do you have a spare?

Knock-Knock.

Who's there?

Candice.

Candice who?

Candice doorbell be reached by cats? Let's see!

Knock-Knock.

Who's there?

Icing.

Icing who?

Icing on your porch! La, la, la!

Knock-Knock.

Who's there?

Wendy.

Wendy who?

Wendy door opens, I'm gonna run inside!

Knock-Knock.

Who's there?

Idol.

Idol who?

Idol you let me in or I'll meow my head off!

Knock-Knock.

Who's there?

Isabelle.

Isabelle who?

Isabelle really a good thing to put on a cat collar? I don't like it.

Knock-Knock!

Who's there?

Fish.

Fish who?

Fish you'd invite me in for a cup of catnip tea!

Knock-Knock.

Who's there?

Catacombs.

Catacombs who?

Catacombs aren't necessary--we use our tongues to brush our fur!

Knock-Knock.

Who's there?

Mister.

Mister who?

Mister flight, so we need somewhere to stay tonight. Won't you let me and the kittens in?

Knock-Knock.

Who's there?

Total.

Total who?

Total the truth, I hope you have some food in there!

Knock-Knock.

Who's there?

Samoa.

Samoa who?

Samoa treats, please! The ones you gave me yesterday were delicious!

Knock-Knock.

Who's there?

Hungary.

Hungary who?

Hungary kitty here, let me in!

Knock-Knock.

Who's there?

Wan.

Wan who?

Wanna invite me in for lunch?

Knock-Knock.

Who's there?

Knead.

Knead who?

Knead a cat to guard your house? I'm the cat for the job!

Knock-Knock.

Who's there?

Nacho.

Nacho who?

Nacho if I have the right house! Does Kevin live here?

Knock-Knock.

Who's there?

Hike.

Hike who?

Why are you talking / About Japanese poems now? / Just let me-ow in!

Knock-Knock.

Who's there?

Chicken.

Chicken who?

Just chicken that you're home. See you later!

Knock-Knock.

Who's there?

Ya.

Ya who?

Oh, you're so excited to see me? How nice!

Knock-Knock.

Who's there?

Beef.

Beef who?

Beef-or my fur gets too soggy, please let me in! There's too much rain!

Knock-Knock.

Who's there?

Taco.

Taco who?

Taco bout a cat-astrophe! My paws are freezing!

Knock-Knock.

Who's there?

App.

App who?

App-arently you don't know how to open a door!

Knock-Knock.

Who's there?

Roach.

Roach who?

Roach you a letter that I was coming over. You got it?

Knock-Knock.

Who's there?

Shore.

Shore who?

Shore could use some food!

Knock-Knock.

Who's there?

Weak.

Weak who?

Weak-ats have been waiting here for hours "Please let us in!"

Knock-Knock.

Who's there?

Claire.

Claire who?

Claire-ly I want to come in. So, hurry up!

Knock-Knock.

Who's there?

Eiffel.

Eiffel who?

Eiffel down and got hurt. Can I have a cuddle?

Knock-Knock.

Who's there?

Wood.

Wood who?

Wood you be my human and take care of me? Meow!

Knock-Knock.

Who's there?

Yam.

Yam who?

Yam a tiny kitten who wants a warm blanket! Do you have one?

Knock-Knock.

Who's there?

Tabby.

Tabby who?

Tabby or not tabby, that is the question!

Knock-Knock.

Who's there?

Maine.

Maine who?

Maine-ly, I want a chin scratch. Maybe some rubs too?

Knock-Knock.

Who's there?

Doom.

Doom who?

Doom me a favor and shine a laser beam out here! I want to play!

Knock-Knock.

Who's there?

Fur.

Fur who?

It's taking fur-ever for you to open the door!

Knock-Knock.

Who's there?

Eight.

Eight who?

Eight you the guy who likes cats? Want to adopt another one?

Knock-Knock.

Who's there?

Five.

Five who?

Five been knocking all day! I need to rest my paws inside.

Knock-Knock.

Who's there?

Four.

Four who?

Four me, can you install a cat door? It would be much easier than this!

Knock-Knock.

Who's there?

Homer.

Homer who?

Homer is where the heart is. Can this be my home, too?

Knock-Knock.

Who's there?

Purr.

Purr who?

Purr-haps you can lend me a soft napping cushion?

Knock-Knock.

Who's there?

Jason.

Jason who?

Jason mice is my favorite hobby. Do you have any inside?

Knock-Knock.

Who's there?

One.

One who?

Once you open the door, I'll tell you!

Knock-Knock.

Who's there?

Furry.

Furry who?

Furry minute you keep me waiting, I'll scratch another piece of your furniture!

Knock-Knock!

Who's there?

Less soap.

Less soap who?

Less soap you like kittens, there's a bunch out here!

Knock-Knock.

Who's there?

Castle.

Castle who?

Castle trip you up if you don't watch where you walk!

Knock-Knock.

Who's there?

Cat who wants to come inside.

Cat who wants to come inside who?

You're not very good at knock-knock jokes, are you?

Knock-Knock.

Who's there?

Meow.

Meow who?

Meow can it take so long to open a door?

Knock-Knock.

Who's there?

Abyssinian.

Abyssinian who?

Abyssinian you around! Bye!

Knock-Knock.

Who's there?

Kent.

Kent who?

Kent you play with me today? Purr-leeze!

Knock-Knock.

Who's there?

Nobel.

Nobel who?

Nobel here, you'd better put one in!

Knock-Knock.

Who's there?

Week.

Week who?

Week can take a cozy nap together once you let me in!

Knock-Knock.

Who's there?

P.

P who?

Hey, I don't smell that bad! Now let me inside!

Knock-Knock.

Who's there?

R.

R who?

R travelling cat choir is the best, let's meow you a song!

Knock-Knock.

Who's there?

Kitten.

Kitten who?

Kitten the car. Let's go to the pet shop for supplies.

Knock-Knock.

Who's there?

Bobtail.

Bobtail who?

Bob, tail me what you're having for dinner! I might stop by later…

Knock-Knock.

Who's there?

Car.

Car who?

Car-pet is better for naps than tile! Just so you know.

Knock-Knock.

Who's there?

Purr.

Purr who?

You have purr-mission to pet me!

Knock-Knock.

Who's there?

Lil.

Lil who?

Lil cats like me won't hurt you! I just want some snuggles!

Knock-Knock.

Who's there?

Trees.

Trees who?

Trees are fun to climb, but now I'm tired! Let me in!

Knock-Knock.

Who's there?

Eye.

Eye who?

Eye really need to use the litter box!

Knock-Knock.

Who's there?

Abel.

Abel who?

Abel to open this door soon? It's really rainy out here!

Knock-Knock.

Who's there?

Beer.

Beer who?

Beer real shame for me to miss my favorite TV show. Let me in!

Knock-Knock.

Who's there?

Wind.

Wind who?

Wind-whos were all closed. So, that's why I'm knocking on your door!

Knock-Knock.

Who's there?

Orange.

Orange who?

Orange you going to let me in? I'm so bored out here!

Knock-Knock.

Who's there?

Puma.

Puma who?

Puma tail and you'll be in trouble! Hisss!

Knock-Knock.

Who's there?

Saber.

Saber who?

Saber excuses for another time. Just open the door!

Knock-Knock.

Who's there?

Catnapped.

Catnapped who?

This catnapped all day, now I'm ready to play!

Knock-Knock.

Who's there?

Cooled.

Cooled who?

Cooled you give me directions to the cat treat store?

Knock-Knock.

Who's there?

Fleece.

Fleece who?

Fleece keep biting me! Can you take me to the vet?

Knock-Knock.

Who's there?

Tooth.

Tooth who?

Tooth be told, I really just want to come inside and purr on your lap!

Knock-Knock.

Who's there?

Concat.

Concat who?

Concat-ulations for making it this far in the book!

Knock-Knock.

Who's there?

Paw.

Paw who?

It's im-paw-sibble to tell so many cat knock-knock jokes in a row!

Knock-Knock.

Who's there?

Cat.

Cat who?

Cat you stop with these jokes!? I'm laughing so hard it hurts!

That's All "Fur" Now!

Wow, you made it to the end of the book. That's PAW-some! How hard did you laugh?

Whenever you're down or bored, come back to this book and read some of your favorite knock-knock jokes. Surely, you'll get a few laughs and giggles out of them!

Who knows, you might even come up with some knock-knock jokes yourself…? So, is that a cat knocking at your door? Are you going to let him in?

Did You Like This Book?

Why don't you leave a review???

Use the link or QR code. Leave as many stars as you like!

Thanks!

https://www.amazon.com/review/create-review/?ie=UTF8&channel=glance-detail&asin=1736763075

Or, scan this QR code…

But purrr-leeze leave a review!

Show that you like crazy cats!!!

Want to Read Other Funny Cat Books?

How about starting with this one….?

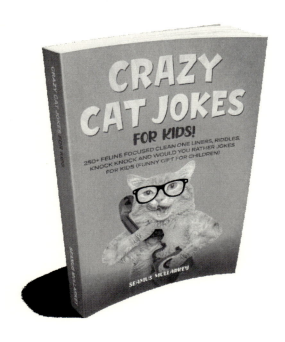

I KNOW YOU LOVE CATS…

I KNOW YOU LOVE BOOKS

WOULDN'T YOU LIKE TO READ MORE FUN BOOKS ABOUT CATS?

FOR FREE…?

WHY NOT JOIN MY FAN CLUB?

SEE ALL THE DETAILS ON THE NEXT PAGE…

Disclaimer

This book is for entertainment purposes only.

The information provided herein is stated to be truthful and consistent, in that any liability, in terms of inattention or otherwise, by any usage or abuse of any policies, processes, or directions contained within is the solitary and utter responsibility of the recipient reader. Under no circumstances will any legal responsibility or blame be held against the publisher for any reparation, damages, or monetary loss due to the information herein, either directly or indirectly.

Made in United States
North Haven, CT
23 June 2023